USA TODAY

CULTURAL MOSAIC

The American Indian Experience

Liz Sonneborn

Twenty-First Century Books · Minneapolis

This book takes a broad look at American Indians. However, like all cultural groups, the American Indian community is extremely diverse. Each member of this community relates to his or her background and heritage in different ways, and each has had a different experience of what it means to be an American Indian.

Twenty-First Century Books
A division of Lerner Publishing Group, Inc.
241 First Avenue North
Minneapolis, MN 55401 U.S.A.

Website address: www.lernerbooks.com

The publisher wishes to thank Ben Nussbaum and Carolina Abood of USA TODAY for their help in preparing this book.

Library of Congress Cataloging-in-Publication Data

Sonneborn, Liz.
    The American Indian Experience / by Liz Sonneborn.
        p.   cm. — (USA TODAY Cultural mosaic)
    Includes bibliographical references and index.
    ISBN 978-0-7613-4086-7 (lib. bdg. : alk. paper)
    1. Indians of North America—Juvenile literature. I. Title.
    E77.4.S618 2011
    970.004'97—dc22   2009007717

Manufactured in the United States of America
1 – DP – 7/15/10

**USA
TODAY®
CULTURAL MOSAIC**

THE FIRST AMERICANS

Tens of thousands of years ago, people migrated from Asia to North America. They walked along a land bridge that then connected the two continents. Over time, these people moved south. They eventually settled all over the Americas. They were the first Americans—American Indians.

American Indians created many different cultures. In North America alone, they lived within about five hundred tribes.

Starting with Christopher Columbus in 1492, non-Indians began traveling to the Americas. These people carried diseases that, over time, killed many American Indians. The newcomers also fought with American Indian tribes. But despite the horrors of disease and war, American Indians survived and retained many of their old customs. At the same time, they adapted to living in a modern, changing world.

In the twenty-first century, American Indians are a vital part of American society. This book will look at who they are, where they've been, and where they're going.

OPPOSITE PAGE: This historical drawing shows Mohawk people doing a day's work.

THIS PAGE: Modern American Indians balance their cultural traditions with twenty-first century life. Here, American Indians in traditional dress display the U.S. and American Indian flags before the start of the Native American Indigenous Games in Denver, Colorado.

CHAPTER 1:
TELLING STORIES

The Cherokees tell stories of Water Beetle. He plunged into the water beneath the sky and brought up the dirt that became Earth. The Shoshones talk of Coyote. He carried humans in a basket and then released them into the world. The Navajos speak of Spider Woman. She taught women the valuable skill of weaving.

For centuries American Indian storytellers have shared many tales, including creation stories such as these. Grandparents told them to their grandchildren. When these children grew up, they shared the same stories with their own grandchildren. They continue to tell these stories as an important part of their heritage.

Among American Indian peoples, stories have always been more than just entertainment. They are also teaching tools. By hearing stories, children

OPPOSITE PAGE: This oil painting shows the Iroquois creation story.

THIS PAGE: An American Indian elder tells stories to the children gathered around him.

learn about their people's history and beliefs. They also find out what is expected of them as members of their tribe. Heroes in the stories show how to behave. The villains show how not to act.

Before American Indians had contact with Europeans and other non-Indians, these stories were told only by word of mouth. American Indians did not write them down. Most American Indian groups did not have a written language.

EARLY WRITINGS

For the most part, American Indians began writing literature only after they learned non-Indian languages. Some of the first texts written by American Indians date from the 1700s. Their authors learned English in schools run by religious organizations. The books were usually about the Christian faith.

In the 1800s, some famous American Indians, such as the Lakota Sioux leader Sitting Bull, "wrote" their life stories. These autobiographies were actually written by non-Indian authors.

Sitting Bull (1831–1890) was a great American Indian spiritual leader.

Writing Cherokee

The Cherokee people originally lived in the southeastern part of what is now the United States. Like most other American Indians, the Cherokee tribe traditionally did not have a way of writing their language. In the early 1800s, one man set out to change that. His name was Sequoyah. Working alone in a cabin, he created a symbol for every sound in the Cherokee language.

Sequoyah decided to teach his writing system to his young daughter Ahyokeh. If she could learn it, adult Cherokees would have no trouble picking it up. To Sequoyah's relief, Ahyokeh learned his system quickly.

Sequoyah started holding shows to demonstrate his invention. He asked Ahyokeh to help him. Sequoyah wrote down messages. Ahyokeh then confidently read them to the crowd. Their audiences were amazed. After these demonstrations, just about every Cherokee wanted to learn Sequoyah's writing system.

In the twenty first century, most Cherokees speak only English. Some, however, can speak the Cherokee language. A few still know how to read and write the Cherokee language using Sequoyah's symbols.

The Cherokee writing system developed by Sequoyah

They were loosely based on the subjects' accounts of their lives, as told to translators. Many of these autobiographies, however, were filled with inaccurate information inserted by the authors.

Probably the first American Indian to write a novel was Cherokee author John Rollin Ridge. Published in 1854, his book was titled *The Life and Adventures of Joaquín Murieta*. It was an exciting story about a Mexican American bandit. In the early twentieth century, a few other American Indians also produced novels. Among the most notable were *Cogewea, the Half-Blood* (1927) by Colville author Mourning Dove and *The Surrounded* (1936) by Cree writer D'Arcy McNickle.

RECENT AMERICAN INDIAN NOVELISTS

For many years, American Indian novelists had a fairly small readership. That changed in 1968, when *House Made of Dawn* was published. Kiowa author N. Scott Momaday wrote this novel. It won Momaday the Pulitzer Prize—one of the greatest honors an American novelist can receive. The novel is considered a classic of American literature.

House Made of Dawn tells the story of Abel, a young American Indian war veteran who comes back to the United States after fighting in World War II (1939–1945). Emotionally wounded by his wartime experiences, Abel finally finds comfort in ancient tribal stories and ceremonies.

N. Scott Momaday's novel *House Made of Dawn* won the Pulitzer Prize in 1969.

www.usatoday.com

USA TODAY

Money

SECTION B

September 20, 2004

From the Pages of USA TODAY

Indian art of storytelling seeps into boardroom; Firms use oral tradition to teach rising executives

As a child, retired Citgo CEO David Tippeconnic sat on the porch of his Oklahoma farmhouse and listened to the stories of his Comanche elders. Tippeconnic, 64, recalls a lesson handed down to his grandfather, to his father and then to himself that he says can be summarized: "Don't trust a red-faced white man."

In business, Tippeconnic has interacted primarily with white men. But he's interpreted the boyhood lesson to mean that he should avoid dealing with anyone, of any race, who angers easily, and that he should maintain his cool. It has served him well. He climbed the ladder at Phillips Petroleum, then served as CEO of Midwestern energy company UNO-VEN from 1995 to 1997, when it was bought by Citgo. He was Citgo's CEO until 2000.

Companies in their never-rest quest for the hot strategy have inadvertently backed into the art of Indian storytelling. While trying everything from Six Sigma [a business management methodology] to Zen [a philosophy that stresses wisdom and enlightenment], they never seemed interested in anything Native American, a culture that does not condone greed. Or, as Indian mystery author Tony Hillerman says, "How do the Navajo tell a witch? They look for somebody who has more than he needs."

That's a rather alien attitude [in the business world]. But Indian storytelling is catching on, whether companies realize it or not. Corporate stories are told by graying boardroom chiefs to intimate groups of up-and-comers. Companies that use it have found it the most effective way to transfer certain knowledge to the next generation.

Companies think they invented knowledge management, but it's something Indians have known for thousands of years, says Wilma Mankiller, ex-chief of the Cherokee Nation in Oklahoma.

There is an obvious clash between the cultures of Native Americans and business, Mankiller says. But they have found a common denominator: Knowledge is valuable, and those who fail to pass it along are dooming others to repeat mistakes.

—Del Jones

Another well-known novel, *Ceremony* (1977) by Laguna Pueblo author Leslie Marmon Silko, also deals with a soldier coming home from World War II. It was the first modern novel written by an American Indian woman.

Momaday and Silko inspired many other American Indian authors to try writing novels. In their works, these novelists explore the struggles of American Indians in the past and present. One of the best-known is James Welch, who was of Blackfoot and Gros Ventre ancestry. His *Fools Crow* (1986) describes how white settlers changed the lives of a band of Blackfoot American Indians in the 1870s. Louise Erdrich is another successful American Indian novelist. A member of the Ojibwe tribe, she has written numerous best-selling books, including *Love Medicine* (1984) and *The Plague of Doves* (2008). Many of her books deal with American Indian people in North Dakota, where she grew up.

WRITING FOR YOUNG PEOPLE

Louise Erdrich is also one of several noted American Indian authors who write for young readers. Among her children's books are *The Birchbark House* (1999) and its two sequels, *The Game of Silence* (2005) and *The Porcupine Year* (2008). The three novels are about an Ojibwe girl named Omakayas growing up in the 1840s and 1850s.

Author Louise Erdrich has written books for adults as well as for young readers. She is a member of the Ojibwe tribe.

USA TODAY
CULTURAL MOSAIC

Joseph Bruchac III is a well-known storyteller and member of the Abenaki tribe. He has written many novels and picture books for children. He is also the author of *Pushing Up the Sky: Seven Native American Plays for Children* (2000).

Lakota Sioux writer Virginia Driving Hawk Sneve is also known for her children's books about American Indians. She has written many novels and histories of specific tribes.

NOTABLE POETS

Many contemporary American Indians write poetry. They are often inspired by traditional songs, which remain an important part of American Indian culture and religion. One such poet is Simon Ortiz. A member of the Acoma Pueblo tribe, he had his first poem published when he was just eleven. He has since written dozens of books of poetry. Creek writer and singer Joy Harjo is another well-known American Indian poet. She has set many of her poems to music. Harjo performs these songs with her band Poetic Justice.

Ofelia Zepeda is one of several American Indian poets who write in their tribal language. A member of the Tohono O'odham tribe, she has published two poetry collections. One of her books, *Jewed 'I-Hoi/Earth Movements* (2005), comes with a CD. On it, Zepeda reads her poems in English and in the Tohono O'odham language.

Zepeda is not only a poet. She is also a linguist (a person who studies human speech and languages).

Ofelia Zepeda, of the Tohono O'odham tribe, writes poetry in her tribal language.

Sherman Alexie

Long a rising star in the world of American Indian literature, Sherman Alexie *(left)* was born in 1966 in Spokane, Washington. His father was of Coeur d'Alene ancestry. His mother was a member of the Spokane tribe.

Alexie grew up on the Spokane Indian Reservation (a tract of land set aside for the Spokane people to live on). When he was born, he had too much fluid in his brain. He had to have brain surgery as a baby and remained sickly for much of his boyhood. Having learned to read at the age of three, Alexie spent most of his time alone, curled up with a book.

Alexie went to college on a scholarship (an award that helps pay for college expenses). At college he began writing fiction and poetry. Alexie has since published more than a dozen volumes of poems and short stories. He has also written several adult novels and the screenplays for the films *Smoke Signals* (1998) and *The Business of Fancydancing* (2002).

Alexie had his greatest popular success in 2007. That year saw the publication of his first novel for young adults, *The Absolutely True Diary of a Part-Time Indian*. The book tells the story of Arnold Spirit Jr., a fourteen-year-old growing up on the Spokane Indian Reservation. Arnold decides to attend a non-reservation high school where the students are all white. There, the other students tease him about his American Indian heritage. Arnold's experiences are based on Alexie's own youth.

The Absolutely True Diary was a big hit with both critics and readers. It won the National Book Award in the Young People's Literature category. Alexie is working on a sequel to *The Absolutely True Diary* that tells of Arnold Spirit's sophomore year in high school.

USA TODAY
CULTURAL MOSAIC

She studies Tohono O'odham and other American Indian languages. In addition to teaching at the University of Arizona in Tucson, Zepeda is the director of the American Indian Language Development Institute. The organization works to preserve American Indian languages, many of which are dying out.

LOSING THEIR LANGUAGES

Before non-Indians arrived, the American Indians of North America spoke about 2,000 different languages. In modern times, approximately 150 American Indian languages are still spoken. Only about 50 of those are known to more than a few people.

The policies of the U.S. government are one reason for the loss of many American Indian languages. Beginning in the 1800s, government officials tried hard to make American Indians give up their old ways. They wanted American Indians to adopt the customs of whites. These officials believed this would help American Indians blend into American society.

As part of this campaign, the government tried to make American Indians stop using their own languages. Instead, they

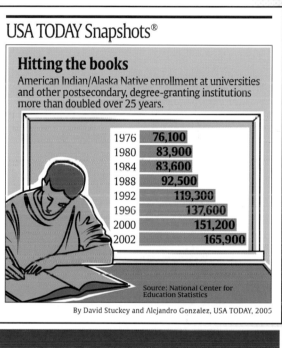

USA TODAY Snapshots®

Hitting the books
American Indian/Alaska Native enrollment at universities and other postsecondary, degree-granting institutions more than doubled over 25 years.

Year	Enrollment
1976	76,100
1980	83,900
1984	83,600
1988	92,500
1992	119,300
1996	137,600
2000	151,200
2002	165,900

Source: National Center for Education Statistics
By David Stuckey and Alejandro Gonzalez, USA TODAY, 2005

In the past, few American Indians had the chance to learn about their languages in college. The number of American Indians enrolled in college is growing, as is the number of classes teaching American Indian languages.

were supposed to speak only English. At government-run schools, American Indian students were punished harshly if they did not obey this rule. Teachers would beat students if they spoke even a word in their own languages.

TEACHING THE NEXT GENERATION

By the late twentieth century, the U.S. government officially changed its position. Scholars convinced the U.S. Congress that it had to act to keep more American Indian languages from being lost. The result was the Native American Languages Act of 1990. The new law stated that American Indian languages are an important part of U.S. culture. It called for these languages to be taught to young American Indians in government-funded programs.

Decades earlier, tribes had already organized efforts to preserve their languages. Some put together dictionaries and grammar books. Others sponsored language classes. These were often taught by elders, because they were the only tribe members who still knew the tribal language.

A few tribes have started schools in which all the lessons are taught in their native languages. One such school is the Arapaho Language Lodge on the Wind River Reservation. The Northern Arapaho tribe of Wyoming operates this school. When the school opened in 2008, the tribe had about eighty-eight hundred members. Only about two hundred knew how to speak Arapaho.

The school was inspired by a speech given five years before by Helen Cedar Tree. In 2003 she was the oldest living Northern Arapaho. She confronted the tribe's council of elders during one of their meetings. "Look at all you guys talking English," she scolded. "[A]nd you know your own language[!] It's like the white man has conquered us."

Ryan Branstetter *(left)*, who is part Walla Walla Indian, learns about the Walla Walla language from instructor Cecilia Bearchum on the Umatilla Indian Reservation in Oregon. A bill passed in the state legislature in 2002 gives tribal elders special licenses to teach in schools.

Her words stirred the Northern Arapaho to action. They became determined to pass on their language to the next generation. Like many other American Indian peoples, they feel that language is central to their tribal identity. Lakota Sioux Ryan Wilson is an American Indian language expert who advised the Northern Arapaho elders. He says, "If [American Indians] lose [our] language, we lose who we are."

CHAPTER 2:

IN THE ARTS

A rt and music have always been a treasured part of American Indian life. For many centuries, American Indian craftspeople have worked with materials they found in nature. From grasses and cedar, they wove baskets. From earth and clay, they molded pots. From soft wood, they carved bowls. From animal skins, they sewed clothing. Most of these practical items were meant to be used by the craftspeople's families. But they were also beautiful objects in which their creators took great pride.

American Indian artisans also traditionally made special

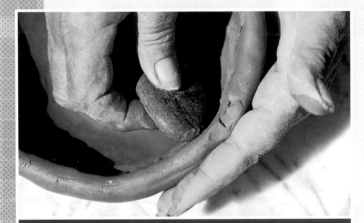

An artist shapes a water drum using a stone at the Cherokee Nation reunion celebration in Cleveland, Tennessee, in 2009. Water drums are used by some American Indians in ceremonies.

objects for ceremonies. Dancers wore decorated clothing and masks. Musicians used rattles, drums, and flutes to accompany ceremonial songs.

In modern times, the works of some professional American Indian artists and musicians reflect their tribes' traditional arts.

This Seminole woman weaves sweetgrass strands into a basket.

Others work in nontraditional art forms, such as painting, sculpture, and rock music. Still others, such as screenwriters and film actors, explore creative fields their ancestors could scarcely have imagined.

MAKING MUSIC

Since the 1800s, non-Indian tourists have visited reservations to hear American Indian musicians and singers. But American Indians did not find a large audience for recordings of their music until the 1960s. At that time, interest in American Indians surged. Both Indians and non-Indians were eager to learn more about American Indian history and culture.

This trend created an unlikely hit album. In 1970 Dakota Sioux actor and musician Floyd Westerman released *Custer Died for Your Sins*. In his songs, Westerman criticized the U.S. government for its history of anti-American Indian policies.

Other American Indian musicians also found success in the 1960s and 1970s. For instance, Jesse Ed Davis, who was of Kiowa-Comanche descent, was a legendary rock and blues guitarist. Another example was Cree performer Buffy Sainte-Marie. She was one of the leading singer-songwriters of the era.

Buffy Sainte-Marie

Buffy Sainte-Marie *(right)* is famous for her music. But she is just as well known as an advocate for American Indian rights. Born Beverly Sainte-Marie in about 1941 on the Piapot Reserve in Saskatchewan, Canada, Sainte-Marie is of Cree descent. She was orphaned as a baby and adopted by a couple in Massachusetts, who gave her the nickname Buffy.

As a girl, Sainte-Marie taught herself how to play the piano and the guitar. To make extra money, she played her own songs in coffeehouses while she attended college. Sainte-Marie studied to become a teacher. But after graduation, she decided to try another career. She moved to New York City to perform in the popular folk music scene of the early 1960s.

Sainte-Marie quickly became a folk star and successful recording artist. Her best-known song was "Universal Soldier," which she recorded in 1964. It became an anthem of antiwar activists protesting the Vietnam War (1957–1975). Sainte-Marie was also famed for her songs about American Indians. She often toured reservation communities and gave generously to American Indian charities.

By the mid-1970s, the popularity of Sainte-Marie's music was dimming. She began to explore other outlets for her creativity. For five years, she appeared on the children's show *Sesame Street*. She also acted in several films and wrote the scores for a few movies. And in 1983, she won an Academy Award for cowriting "Up Where We Belong," a song from the popular movie *An Officer and a Gentleman*.

From her home studio in Hawaii, Sainte-Marie continues to record music. She also uses computers to create digital art. In many of her works, she adds color and other elements to nineteenth-century photographs of American Indians.

USA TODAY
CULTURAL MOSAIC

CONTEMPORARY MUSICIANS

Several American Indian performers have made their mark in new age music (a soft, instrumental form of music meant to inspire relaxation and peacefulness). R. Carlos Nakai, of Navajo-Ute descent, has been particularly successful. He is considered the foremost American Indian flutist. Nakai has performed in concert halls around the world.

Oneida singer and guitarist Joanne Shenandoah also has a worldwide following. Shenandoah writes many of her own songs. They often blend traditional Iroquois music with the contemporary sounds of pop and country.

Rita Coolidge was a popular singer of the 1970s. She recently embarked on a second career as part of the trio Walela. Named after the Cherokee word for "hummingbird," the group mixes rock with American Indian rhythms played on the drum and flute.

Some American Indian musicians work in newer musical styles. The group Robby Bee and the Boyz from the Rez is known for its hip-hop sound. The Cherokee actor Litefoot is also an acclaimed rap artist. He tours frequently, visiting American Indian reservations across the United States.

R. Carlos Nakai performs his instrumental music at a gathering in 2005.

Nammys and Grammys

The diversity of the American Indian music business is on display each year at the Native American Music Awards. The awards, nicknamed the Nammys, recognize excellence in a wide range of musical styles, from traditional American Indian music to gospel to rock. Recent winners include new age artist Carroll Medicine Crow, country singer Tracy Bone, and the reggae band Native Roots. Since 2001 American Indian music has also been honored at the Grammy Awards. Each year one lucky recording artist or producer takes home the Grammy for Best Native American Music Album. Recent winners include Johnny Whitehorse for *Totemic Flute Chants*, Mary Youngblood for *Dance with the Wind*, and Jim Wilson for *Sacred Ground: A Tribute to Mother Earth*.

TRADITIONAL ARTS

Many modern American Indian artists create traditional craftwork for sale, usually to non-Indians. These wares are not only popular among U.S. collectors. People the world over treasure the work of traditional American Indian artists.

The Navajos are particularly revered as artists. Many Navajo men are great jewelry makers. Their trademark is silver jewelry adorned with turquoise stones. For more than a century, Navajo women have been known for weaving beautiful wool rugs. They are decorated with colorful, vibrant patterns, often formed from diamond or zigzag shapes. Some weavers color their yarn with commercial dyes. Others prefer the subtle colors of vegetable dyes that they make themselves.

The Hopi and other Pueblo tribes are famous for their pottery.

USA TODAY
CULTURAL MOSAIC

By the late twentieth century, Pueblo potters such as Maria Martinez and Margaret Tafoya were considered among the most skillful pottery makers in the entire world. Many modern potters have followed in their footsteps. In fact, at least seventy-five members of the Tafoya family are professional potters.

American Indian artisans across the United States make baskets for sale. California tribes are particularly respected for their basketmaking skills. Often their woven treasures are decorated with feathers. California basket makers also like to show off their skills by making tiny baskets—some as small as a thumbnail.

Some American Indian craftspeople still practice the art of quillwork. They decorate objects with tiny stitches, using dyed and flattened porcupine quills as their thread. A related craft is beadwork. It produces similar decorations from manufactured glass beads. Creek artist Marcus Amerman offers a

USA TODAY Snapshots®

Top 'Roadshow' treasures

PBS' *Antiques Roadshow* is now in its 10th season. Top appraisals featured on the air:

Navajo blanket (19th century), Tucson, $350,000-$500,000

James E. Buttersworth painting (19th century), Tampa, $250,000-$500,000

Seymour card table (18th century), Secaucus, N.J., $200,000-$300,000

Ruby and diamond jewelry (early 20th century), Richmond, Va., $257,000

Tang dynasty statue (sixth-ninth century), Albuquerque, $120,000-$250,000

Source: Antiques Roadshow/WGBH Boston

By Tracey Wong Briggs and Keith Simmons, USA TODAY, 2006

American Indian craftwork is treasured by collectors. A Navajo blanket was recently deemed the most valuable item on an episode of *Antiques Roadshow* on public television.

contemporary twist on beadworking. He uses beadwork to re-create photographs. Some show American Indians from the 1800s. Others show comic-book characters or celebrities.

BLENDING OLD AND NEW

For decades, many American Indians have embraced nontraditional ways of making art. They may paint, sculpt, or take photographs. Among the giants of nontraditional American Indian art is Chiricahua Apache sculptor Allan Houser. During his career, he created about one thousand large-scale sculptures from stone, wood, and bronze. Many depict abstract figures of American Indian people. Two years before his death in 1994, Houser became the first American Indian to receive the National Medal of Arts.

Houser was more than an artist. He was also a teacher. For many years, he taught art students at the Institute of American Indian Arts (IAIA) in Santa Fe, New Mexico. This school has trained many leading American Indian artists. It also operates a museum that displays exhibits of contemporary work.

Another influential teacher at IAIA was Luiseño painter Fritz Scholder. He was best known for his bold portraits of American Indians that combined old and new elements. One of his most famous paintings is *Super Indian No. 2*. It shows an American Indian dancer in ceremonial dress eating an ice cream cone.

Many American Indian artists have used their work to comment on their heritage. Maidu painter Harry Fonseca was known for his playful images of Coyote, a character in many traditional American Indian stories. Santa Clara Pueblo potter Nora Naranjo-Morse is famous for her life-size clay sculptures of Pearlene. Through this character, she explores how American Indian women adapt to new

The National Museum of the American Indian

On September 21, 2004, twenty thousand American Indians from about five hundred tribes gathered on the National Mall in Washington, D.C. They were there for the opening of the National Museum of the American Indian. This enormous museum is devoted to the art, history, and literature of American Indian peoples. Its collection includes more than eight hundred thousand objects made and used by tribes throughout the United States and Canada. Its exhibitions not only explore the way American Indians lived long ago. Many shows also examine contemporary American Indian life. Recent exhibitions have also showcased the works of modern American Indian artists, such as James Luna (Luiseño), R. C. Gorman (Navajo), and Fritz Scholder (Luiseño).

This bronze statue by artist Allan Houser is featured at the National Museum of the American Indian.

experiences and changing times. One Pearlene sculpture shows Pearlene teaching her more traditional cousins how to play poker. Mohawk photographer Shelley Niro gained renown for her "Mohawks in Beehives" series. In these photos, her three sisters appear in flashy dresses and hairstyles. Their assertiveness challenges the stereotype of American Indian women as weak victims.

AMERICAN INDIANS ON FILM

Since the birth of moviemaking, American Indians have often been depicted on film. They have always been a central part of Westerns—movies that deal with the American West in the late 1800s. Westerns were especially popular in the mid-twentieth century. But at that time, the American Indian characters in Westerns were almost always villains. Usually, these characters were not even played by American Indians. In fact, very few American Indians ever appeared onscreen in the mid-1900s.

But just as they were in music and visual art, the 1960s and 1970s were a period of change for American Indians in the movies. A few moviemakers began to rethink the Western. They tried something new. They made American Indians the heroes. *Little Big Man* (1970) was one of these new Westerns. It was also notable for its casting. Some of the American Indian parts were played by American Indian actors. A starring role went to Chief Dan George, the leader of the Tsleil-Waututh Nation. George portrayed a wise Cheyenne elder named Old Lodge Skins. For his moving and funny performance, George was nominated for an Academy Award. He was the first American Indian so honored.

DANCES WITH WOLVES

Since then two other American Indians have received Academy Award nominations. In 1975 Creek actor Will Sampson was nominated for his supporting role in *One Flew Over the Cuckoo's Nest*. He played a mentally ill patient named Chief Bromden. In 1990 Graham Greene of the Oneida tribe was honored for his part in *Dances with Wolves*. He played the quiet yet forceful Lakota Sioux leader Kicking Bird.

Kevin Costner *(left)* and Graham Greene in a scene from *Dances with Wolves* (1990). Greene was nominated for an Academy Award for his role in the film, which went on to win the Academy Award for Best Picture.

Dances with Wolves featured many other American Indian actors as well, including Rodney A. Grant (Omaha), Tantoo Cardinal (Métis), and Floyd Westerman. In portions of the film, actors speak the Lakota Sioux language. Many American Indians felt the film was a great step forward for the depiction of American Indians onscreen. But some felt the movie went too far in trying to reshape the Western. They criticized the movie for portraying Indians as too good and too wise. They wished for Indian characters that were a little less noble and a little more realistic.

Nevertheless, *Dances with Wolves* was a big hit at the box office. It was also a favorite with critics. The movie won an Academy Award for Best Picture. For American Indians in the film industry, *Wolves*'s success marked an important turning point. Suddenly, Hollywood not only wanted to make movies about American Indians. It also wanted to cast them with American Indian actors.

www.usatoday.com

News

SECTION A

March 25, 1991

From the Pages of USA TODAY

Hollywood's chance to get beyond the cliches of Western myth

For most of the 20th century, when Indians attacked the cavalry, the audience thought, "Oh, no!" In *Dances With Wolves*, when Indians attack the cavalry, the audience thinks, "Thank heavens!"

Making the shift from "Oh, what a mess, the Indians are attacking," to "Oh, what a relief, the Indians are attacking," is a stretching exercise for the mind. That flexibility, in turn, permits Americans to face the fact that this nation originated in invasion and conquest.

With gifts not found in the average Western American historian, [*Dances With Wolves* actor and director] Kevin Costner has been a valuable messenger, carrying a vital lesson on conquest to a wide audience. On that count, and a number of others, I'm ready to join—or, first, found—the Western History Association Chapter of the Kevin Costner Fan Club. So, Hollywood, don't stop here. Join the cause of the re-exploration of the American West. Consider, for instance, the stories of the majority of native people on this continent, people who were not horse-riding, buffalo-hunting Plains Indians.

Consider the Indian people who fished and hunted by canoe in the Pacific Northwest, or the Indian people today who, as lawyers, have taken up the causes seemingly settled in battles a century ago.

Consider the moral complexity of white people involved in the conquest, people who were rarely as simple as the white wretches staffing the Western Army in *Dances With Wolves*. Undersupplied, underequipped and frequently poorly led, Western soldiers were unlikely saints and unlikely villains—often European immigrants or African-American freedmen desperate for jobs.

So what follows *Dances With Wolves*? Can Hollywood really dig its way out from the avalanche of stereotypes it unleashed upon the West in the 20th century? The great Western writer Wallace Stegner has invited Americans to move beyond the old, tired myths of the West and to "dream other dreams—and better." Designer and distributor of dreams, Hollywood may well decide whether we say yes or no to that invitation. *Dances With Wolves*, along with its enthusiastic audience response, suggests that our answer might be yes.

—Patricia Nelson Limerick,
from the Opinion page

ONSCREEN AND BEHIND THE CAMERA

In recent years, the movie business has embraced a new generation of American Indian stars. In addition to appearing in *Dances with Wolves*, Cherokee actor Wes Studi found meaty roles in *The Last of the Mohicans* (1992) and *The New World* (2005). Best known as the voice of the title character of Disney's animated *Pocahontas* (1995), Inuit-Cree Irene Bedard has also appeared on television in the movie *Lakota Woman: Siege at Wounded Knee* (1994) and the miniseries *Into the West* (2005). Perhaps the most famous American Indian actor of recent years is Adam Beach. An Ojibwe, Beach was the star of the films *Windtalkers* (2002) and *Flags of Our Fathers* (2006). He also appeared in *Bury My Heart at Wounded Knee*, which won an Emmy Award for Outstanding Made for Television Movie in 2007.

Increasingly, American Indians are making their mark behind the camera as well. Many would-be American Indian directors and screenwriters have received a helping hand from the Sundance Institute. This organization has a program for American Indians seeking careers in film. The program's alumni include Sherman Alexie and Chris Eyre. In the film world, Alexie is best known as the writer and director of *The Business of Fancydancing*. Eyre has directed several well-received features, including Alexie's *Smoke Signals* and a film called *Skins*—a 2002 picture based on a novel by Lovelock Paiute author Adrian C. Louis.

Most films about Indians made by non-Indians deal with Indians of the past. Indian directors such as Alexie and Eyre, however, are more interested in portraying the struggles and challenges of modern American Indians. Their pioneering work is reimagining Hollywood's view of American Indian peoples. For the first time onscreen, mainstream viewers are seeing American Indian life from an American Indian perspective.

CHAPTER 3:
SPORTS AND GAMES

American Indians are proud of their athletic traditions. Throughout history, physical competitions have given people a way to relax and spend time together. Like other peoples, American Indians also played sports to keep their bodies and minds strong and healthy.

Native peoples of the United States and Canada first invented early versions of canoeing, sledding, kayaking, and field hockey. These sports are still played in the twenty-first century.

This mid-1800s painting shows American Indians playing a ball game similar to lacrosse. The painting was created by American artist Seth Eastman.

PLAYING BALL

In North America, the most popular traditional American Indian sports were ball games. These games usually involved two teams of players. Each player had a stick or racket. Players scored points by using their rackets to hit a ball into the other team's goal.

Traditional American Indian ball games inspired the modern sport

A member of the Iroquois Nationals makes a play at the World Indoor Lacrosse Championship in 2007.

of lacrosse. These days, both Indians and non-Indians play lacrosse. In fact, lacrosse is one of the fastest-growing sports in the world.

The Iroquois are particularly passionate about lacrosse. They have their own international lacrosse team, the Iroquois Nationals. In 2007 the Nationals came in second in the World Indoor Lacrosse Championship. The team is a great source of pride for its fans.

BILLY MILLS AND JIM THORPE

Many American Indian groups are known for their skills as runners. Especially in the Southwest, young American Indian men traditionally ran great distances as a display of their strength and character. Young American Indian athletes continue this tradition by joining their schools' track-and-field teams.

The best-known American Indian runner is Billy Mills. A member of the Lakota Sioux tribe, he won a gold medal in the 10,000-meter race at the 1964 Olympics. The next year, he set a world record for the 6-mile (10-kilometer) run.

The most famous American Indian Olympian, however, is Sac and Fox athlete Jim Thorpe. In 1904, as a teenager, Thorpe attended Carlisle Indian School—a boarding school for American Indians.

American Indian Team Names and Mascots

In Kansas City, Missouri, football fans cheer on the Chiefs. In Atlanta, Georgia, baseball enthusiasts root for the Braves. In Washington, D.C., football lovers shout their support for the Redskins. Since the early 1900s, many teams have named themselves with terms such as these, which refer to American Indians.

The names are controversial, however. The teams say the names are a tribute to American Indians. They claim the names celebrate the physical strength and fighting spirit of American Indians. Many Indians, however, disagree. They find the names insulting. They feel the names spread the stereotype of Indians as savage and primitive.

Many teams also have Indian mascots. For instance, the uniforms of the Cleveland Indians baseball team picture Chief Wahoo. This cartoonish character is a red-faced man with a big grin and a feather in his hair. Many American Indians are offended by Chief Wahoo. Activists have gone to court to try to stop the team's use of Chief Wahoo as its mascot.

Not all American Indians object to Indian team names and mascots. The Seminoles, for example, are pleased that the Florida State University football team is named after their tribe. The tribe even helped design the costume and face paint worn by the team's mascot, Chief Osceola.

Chief Osceola, the mascot for Florida State University's football team, was designed with the help and approval of the Seminole American Indians.

There, he ran track and field, played football and baseball, and even competed in ballroom dancing.

With Thorpe leading the way, the Carlisle football team became a phenomenon. Its players were some of the best anywhere. They went up against teams from prestigious schools, such as Harvard University and the University of Chicago. Often, Carlisle's opponents ridiculed the American Indian team. But the Carlisle players usually won.

At the 1912 Olympics in Stockholm, Sweden, Thorpe won two gold medals. He earned them in two very demanding track-and-field competitions—the pentathlon and the decathlon. The pentathlon includes five events. The decathlon involves ten.

During the medals ceremony, Sweden's King Gustav said to Thorpe, "Sir, you are the greatest athlete in the world." Thorpe responded simply with "Thanks, King." Many people still regard Thorpe as one of the best American athletes ever.

AMERICAN INDIANS AT THE OLYMPICS

In addition to Mills and Thorpe, about a dozen other American Indians have competed in the Olympics. For example, Naomi Lang of the Karuk people competed at the 2002 Winter Games in Salt Lake City, Utah. She received a standing ovation for her ice dancing routine. Other Indian competitors at the Olympics have included runners, basketball players, hockey stars, and even one judo champion. The judo competitor was Northern Cheyenne athlete Ben Nighthorse Campbell. After competing in the 1964 Olympics, he served as a member of the U.S. Congress from 1993 until 2005.

Making the Olympic team, however, seems an impossible dream to many talented young American Indians. They often do not have enough money to afford years of intensive training. Raising the money can be difficult. In 2007 Maurice Smith of the Native American Sports Council explained to *USA Today* the problems of one American Indian Olympic hopeful, Navajo runner Brandon Leslie. Smith said, "I can't raise a dollar for this kid because nobody believes in his passion and understands here's the next Billy Mills."

ALL-INDIAN COMPETITIONS

So far, all American Indian Olympians have represented the United States. But some American Indians want to change that. They want American Indian nations to band together and field their own Olympic team.

American Indians already do have their own version of the Olympics. It is called the North American Indigenous Games. At this event, American Indian athletes from all over the United States and Canada compete. During the 2008 games, six thousand participants competed in sixteen events. They included traditional activities, such as lacrosse and canoeing. Non-Indian sports included soccer and tae kwon do.

For decades, Alaska has hosted the World Eskimo-Indian Olympics. The event features many sports unique to the native peoples of Alaska. These sports emphasize the physical traits needed to survive in Alaska's harshest environments.

One such event is the knuckle hop. It tests athletes' strength. Participants lie down in a "push-up" position. With only their knuckles and toes touching the ground, they hop forward. The winner is the player who hops the farthest before giving out.

In the northwestern United States, tribes come together each year for the Tribal Journey. Held annually since 1997, this celebration has revived the almost-lost art of dugout canoeing. For centuries American Indians of the Northwest traveled the waters of the Pacific Ocean in handcrafted canoes. They were made by digging out the middle of great cedar logs. The Tribal Journey teaches young tribespeople how to make and navigate these traditional vessels.

AT THE RODEO

During the 1800s, American Indians of the Great Plains were known for their horse riding skills. For example, Great Plains horsemen hunted herds of buffalo. Buffalo hunts provided many American Indian families with food and with materials for many everyday items.

In the 1800s, battles were commonly fought by soldiers on horses. So when Great Plains warriors battled with other tribes or with the U.S. Army, they often did so on horseback.

In modern times, American Indians of the Plains show off their horse riding talents at rodeos. Throughout the West, dozens of all-Indian rodeos are held each year. Every fall, the best rodeo riders compete at the National Indian Finals Rodeo Championship.

All-Indian rodeos are popular with Native peoples and non-Indians alike. Large crowds gather to watch contestants compete in events such as calf roping, steer wrestling, and bareback riding. Most competitors are men—but some events feature only women riders. At some rodeos, children show off their horsemanship. Boys and girls as young as eight might ride steers or rope small calves.

PROFESSIONAL SPORTS

Many American Indians love watching and playing baseball, basketball, football, and other non-Indian sports. A few talented American Indian athletes have turned professional. They include Navajo golfer Notah Begay III, Cherokee bowler Mike Edwards, and Nomlaki baseball pitcher Kyle Lohse.

Yet few young American Indians play on college and professional teams. Players for these teams are usually recruited in high school. American Indian students have a high dropout rate. Even star athletes often leave school before recruiters can spot them. In addition, recruiters rarely visit the remote reservation schools that many American Indian students attend.

Making a career in sports may be hard for young American Indians. But within their own communities, skilled athletes are celebrated. Especially in the western United States, high school basketball players are heroes within their tribes. At each game, the bleachers are filled with friends and relatives cheering them on.

From the Pages of USA TODAY

Begay: New face of golf, Rising star, Tour's first full Native American

Golfer Notah Begay III belies [contradicts] the notion that the PGA Tour [a group that operates professional golf tours] is the private playground of country-club clones.

Begay, 27, like his former Stanford [University] teammates Tiger Woods and Casey Martin, is breaking down barriers and shattering stereotypes. [He] is believed to be the first full-blooded Native American member of the Tour.

"Hopefully, some young kid who doesn't know what he wants to do can look at me and see hope," says Begay, a two-time winner in 1999, who will tee it up in today's first round of the season-opening Mercedes Championships on Maui [in Hawaii].

Begay wants to break down stereotypes—namely, that all Native Americans speak broken English, wear feathered headdresses and live on reservations. "I take it as a challenge to educate people," says Begay, whose first name is pronounced NO-tuh and means "almost there" in Navajo (his last name is pronounced Bih-GAY).

As a youngster, Begay spent time living in a small adobe house on the Isleta Pueblo Reservation near Albuquerque [New Mexico], his birthplace. "For a while, we had to boil hot water on a stove to take a bath," he recalls.

Begay refused to feel sorry for himself. He made the most of it, even though his parents divorced when he was young.

His first victory, at the Reno-Tahoe Open [in Nevada] in August, attracted a lot of attention. His friend, Olympic champ Billy Mills, who is half Sioux, was there the final day. "I want to be there when Notah wins his first major championship," says Mills, winner of the 10,000 meters at the 1964 Olympics in Tokyo [Japan].

He's already a celebrity in his native Southwest. Albuquerque mayor Jim Baca proclaimed last Nov. 12 "Notah Begay Day." "Notah definitely stands out," Martin says. "He's so different from the normal born-and-bred country-club player."

—Harry Blauvelt

Kids play three-on-three basketball games at the Navajo reservation in Arizona. Basketball is very popular at schools on reservations.

Basketball teams are important at reservation schools. These schools usually do not have much money. Basketball is a great game because it doesn't require expensive equipment. In addition, for many American Indian students, basketball games offer an opportunity to challenge the prejudices of some of their white neighbors, who regard Indians as inferior. By playing the best game they can, they can show their pride in their talent and in their culture.

THE STORY OF SUANNE BIG CROW

SuAnne Big Crow was one such student. Her pride and courage helped change her community. A Lakota Sioux, Big Crow grew up on the Pine Ridge Reservation in South Dakota. She was a star student and athlete. Big Crow liked all sports, but she especially loved basketball. Her high school team was the Lady Thorpes, named after the great American Indian athlete Jim Thorpe.

In 1988 the team traveled to the nearby town of Lead for a game. Before the Lady Thorpes took the court, the largely white crowd began yelling anti-American Indian slurs. The players became nervous as they listened to the ugly remarks from the locker room. They had no idea what the crowd might do when they came out to play.

Big Crow decided to take action. Alone, she ran onto the center court. Big Crow took off her warm-up jacket and swung it around her as she performed the traditional shawl dance. While dancing, she sang a Lakota song. Her brave display silenced the crowd. The once-hostile audience was stunned by the young woman's courage and grace.

SuAnne Big Crow

In 1992 Big Crow was killed in a car accident. But people on Pine Ridge and beyond still remember her fondly. Like many other American Indian sports stars, she instilled a lasting sense of pride in her people.

In 2002 the SuAnne Big Crow Boys and Girls Club opened in the town of Pine Ridge. The facility is more than an athletic center. It is also a source of inspiration for young Lakotas. Through photographs and videos of SuAnne, they can learn about how this great student athlete became a great hero as well.

CHAPTER 4:

THE SPIRITUAL WORLD

Like their ancestors, modern American Indians hold a wide variety of spiritual beliefs. These beliefs differ from tribe to tribe and even from community to community.

The traditional spiritual beliefs of American Indian peoples do have some common elements, however. For instance, American Indians tend to see a close connection between the physical world and the spiritual world. They often believe sacred power is everywhere. It is found in everything, from humans to trees to rocks to rivers.

For this reason, American Indian religions honor nature. Traditionally, Indians performed ceremonies and sang songs as part of their worship to please spirits that protected their environment. These American Indians saw the land and the creatures in it as precious.

In modern times, too, spirituality is part of everyday life for many

A Navajo medicine man (spiritual healer) performs a ceremony with eagle feathers while standing near a hogan (a traditional Navajo dwelling).

American Indians. Throughout the day, they may say prayers associated with different tasks. For instance, some American Indians, as soon as they wake up, thank the creator for the new day. In addition, American Indian groups often set aside certain times each year for specific ceremonies. These events allow people to come together to celebrate and give thanks to the spirit realm.

Many books have been written about American Indian religions. But traditionally, American Indians' spiritual beliefs were not passed along in a written text. Instead, each generation taught the next about the group's beliefs. Elders still share with young people the old stories, songs, and prayers. In this way, American Indians have kept their religious traditions alive.

Sand Paintings

American Indian spiritual leaders in the southwestern United States sometimes make sand paintings as part of a ceremony or healing ritual. They typically create these images from colored sands, powdered roots or bark, and flower and corn pollen. These materials are used to "paint" supernatural beings and sacred symbols. Sand paintings may look like works of art. But they are not meant to last. They are always destroyed after the ceremony ends.

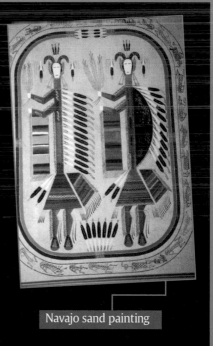

Navajo sand painting

AMERICAN INDIANS AND CHRISTIANITY

In the 1800s, non-Indian missionaries (religious teachers) introduced Christianity to Indian peoples. Missionaries were mostly priests and ministers who came to American Indian communities to convert the people there. Many American Indians adopted Christianity. But not all of them gave up their old ways. They found ways of blending the two religious traditions. American Indians still often blend traditions in modern times.

Some American Indians practice religions that formally combine Christian and traditional Indian beliefs. One example is the Indian Shaker religion. A Coast Salish man named John Slocum founded this faith in 1881. Slocum fell very ill, but when his wife, Mary, began shaking uncontrollably, he recovered. Slocum believed he was healed by her shaking, which was caused by a divine power. Slocum then began to tell others about his religious beliefs. Soon his ideas were embraced by tribespeople in Washington; Oregon; California; and British Columbia, Canada. Some communities still practice the Indian Shaker religion. Church services may include some Christian elements, such as crosses, candles and, among some congregrations, reading of the Bible.

Another modern American Indian religion that combines elements of traditional practice with Christianity is the Native American Church. It began in the late 1800s. Then certain religious ideas of American Indians in the Southwest and Mexico spread to present-day Oklahoma. These ideas included eating peyote as a religious act. Peyote is a part of the mescal cactus. Eating peyote causes people to have visions.

The great Comanche leader Quanah Parker, like many other western Indians, adopted the peyote ceremony. Its teachings spread

USA TODAY CULTURAL MOSAIC

to many tribes in the central United States. In
modern times, about 250,000 people belong
to the Native American Church. They
believe that the peyote ceremony allows
them to communicate with God and with
Jesus. As Parker famously explained, non-
Indians go to church to talk about Jesus. Indians
attend peyote ceremonies to talk with Jesus.

RELIGIOUS FREEDOM

In the late 1800s, the U.S. government outlawed
some American Indian religious practices. American
Indians could go to jail if they were caught performing
traditional ceremonies, attending an Indian Shaker
church service, or taking peyote.

Peyote use remained illegal in many states well
into the late twentieth century. The Native American
Church fought in court for change. In 1994 the U.S.
Congress amended, or changed, the American Indian
Religious Freedom Act. The amendment legalized the use of peyote
during American Indian religious ceremonies across the United States.
Members of the Native American Church could at last practice their
religion without fear of being arrested.

In the 1990s, Congress also addressed other issues that limited
American Indians' freedom of religion. For example, many museums have American Indian ceremonial objects in their collections.

www.usatoday.com

News

SECTION A

August 11, 1994

From the Pages of USA TODAY

'Good medicine' vs. the law: Indians are winning right to use peyote

Native Americans are poised to expand their First Amendment rights. The [U.S.] Senate is expected to soon approve a bill that lifts the last barriers to Native American use of peyote in religious ceremonies. The House [of Representatives] passed a similar measure earlier this week.

· Indian leaders call this fight over the ancient ceremony the first test of President Clinton's vows last spring to bolster Native American rights. Clinton supports legalization and the Justice Department calls it "an important protection for the exercise of Native American religions." The Drug Enforcement Administration and dozens of church leaders support lifting restrictions, yet 22 states still forbid peyote.

"So now a North Dakota church member could drive to Texas to buy peyote (legally), and could be arrested in Nebraska," says Robert Peregoy of the Native American Rights Fund. "What other religion has to carry a grid map around?"

The crisis mounted in 1990 when the Supreme Court ruled the First Amendment [to the U.S. Constitution] does not protect sacramental use of peyote. "We are indigenous people. This country was

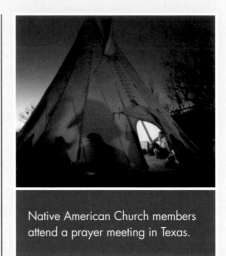

Native American Church members attend a prayer meeting in Texas.

founded on the same reason, equality," says Navajo Frank Dayash Jr., a Maryland NASA employee and regional Native American Church officer. "But we could be put in prison for praying."

Indian use of peyote goes back at least 10,000 years. "It's a real good medicine," says Abraham Spotted Elk Sr., a Cheyenne. "When it's in your system, you start thinking of the creator."

Unless Congress approves peyote use, Spotted Elk says, "it seems like we have to live with fear all the time."

—Linda Kanamine

These items were bought or stolen from tribes a long time ago. Museums may display them as pieces of art. But to American Indians, they are sacred objects and are not meant to be in museums. A federal law, passed in 1990, allows American Indian tribes to reclaim these objects so they can once again use them in ceremonies.

PRESERVING SACRED SITES

During the 1800s, federal and state governments took over large areas of Indian land in the United States. Often these areas included sacred sites. These are places that an American Indian group considers especially holy. Certain ceremonies and rituals can be properly performed only at such sacred sites.

Ever since, American Indians have worked hard to take back their sacred sites. Sometimes they have succeeded. In the 1970s, for instance, the Taos Pueblos convinced the U.S. government to return part of the sacred Blue Lake to their control.

In the twenty-first century, the Western Apaches are trying to protect sacred Mount Graham in Arizona. The sky above this mountain

Observatories can be seen near Mount Graham in Arizona. The Western Apaches want to remove the buildings from land they consider sacred.

Eagle Feathers

Since 1940 it has been illegal for Americans to own eagle feathers. The law is meant to protect eagles, which are a treasured symbol of the United States. But some American Indians use eagle feathers in traditional ceremonies. So the U.S. government established the National Eagle Repository near Denver, Colorado. The repository collects feathers from dead eagles. American Indians can use the feathers in religious ceremonies without breaking the law.

is extremely clear. For this reason, the U.S. government has allowed several organizations to construct observatories in the area. For many years, the Western Apaches have protested the observatories. They believe the buildings spoil this sacred land.

AMERICAN INDIANS AND THE NEW AGE MOVEMENT

In recent years, many non-Indians have become fascinated by traditional American Indian religions. Some have adopted American Indian beliefs. These people are often involved with the New Age movement. The New Age movement accepts spiritual beliefs from many different cultures and religions, including those of American Indians.

American Indians do not always welcome this interest in their religious beliefs. For one thing, New Age believers frequently crowd sacred American Indian sites. Some also travel to American Indian communities to find a leader who will share religious wisdom. But many American Indians do not want to instruct outsiders about their religious beliefs. They feel their sacred knowledge is best kept within their tribe.

American Indians are also offended by non-Indians who pose as Indian healers and religious figures. Many of these non-Indians write books and lead seminars to make money from their teachings. American Indians tend to dismiss such people as "plastic medicine men," or false religious healers. In the eyes of American Indians, religion is not about making money. They view this approach as disrespectful and disturbing. As Matthew King, a Lakota Sioux spiritual leader, once explained, "For someone who has not learned how our balance is maintained to pretend to be a medicine man is very, very dangerous."

CHAPTER 5:

CEREMONIES AND HOLIDAYS

I n traditional American Indian society, when people gathered, it was often for a ceremony. Ceremonies were not only an expression of American Indians' religious beliefs. They were also a way of uniting a community and reminding its people of their shared values.

Throughout much of U.S. history, American Indians were discouraged or even prohibited from performing traditional ceremonies. But American Indians fought to preserve this vital part of their culture. As a result, many ceremonies survived and are still performed.

MARKING MILESTONES

Some American Indian ceremonies celebrate a milestone in a person's life. For example, an American Indian community might hold a ceremony when a baby is born, a child is given a name, or a couple gets married.

OPPOSITE PAGE: A Shoshone man performs a fancy dance at an American Indian festival and powwow in Idaho.

THIS PAGE: A couple gets married in an Algonquin wedding ceremony in Quebec, Canada.

Many ceremonies mark a young person's growth into adulthood. One of the most common is the vision quest. Vision quests remain an important rite of passage for the Crows and other western tribes. On a vision quest, a youth of about the age of twelve goes into the wilderness alone for several days to experience the spirit world. The youth usually prepares for this journey by consulting with elders.

Other ceremonies are meant to ensure a successful home life. The Navajos, for example, hold a house blessing when someone builds a hogan. During the ceremony, this traditional Navajo dwelling is sprinkled with sacred cornmeal while the Navajo participants pray and sing.

A young girl takes part in a Sunrise Dance with other members of her Apache tribe in Arizona. Her face is painted with a mixture of clay and cornmeal. The ceremony is held to prepare girls for adulthood.

Healing Veterans

Many tribes have ceremonies to heal soldiers returning from war. These ceremonies provide comfort and help American Indian veterans readjust to their lives back home. The U.S. Department of Veterans Affairs has recognized the effectiveness of these ceremonies. During the Iraq war, which began in 2003, the department started working with tribes in New Mexico. At veterans'

American Indian veterans *(right)* take part in a ceremony in Utah to help them heal after war.

hospitals throughout the state, returning soldiers were given the chance to participate in traditional healing rites overseen by American Indian spiritual leaders. One such leader was Alfred Gibson, a medicine man who performed the Navajo Enemy Way ritual. As he explained it, "the Enemy Way ceremony rejuvenates [the veterans]. The songs, prayers, drumming, and herbs we use cleanse the body from the effects of war."

ENSURING GOOD FORTUNE

Some ceremonies are performed to offer thanks for a group's good fortune and well-being. Each summer, for example, the Cherokees and other southeastern tribes hold the Green Corn Ceremony when the first ear of the year's corn crop ripens. By performing the ceremony, these tribes give thanks for the upcoming harvest. The Green Corn Ceremony is also a time of renewal. People clean their houses and settle old arguments. Like New Year's Day, it offers a chance to make a fresh start.

Many tribes in the Northwest hold a First Salmon Ceremony to honor the first salmon caught in the spring. After the fish is cooked and eaten, its bones are returned to the water. Through the ritual, the tribes show respect for the salmon, which traditionally was a major part of their diet.

The Lakota Sioux still hold the Sun Dance each year in the summer. During this ceremony, the Lakotas sing, dance, and fast. They also give thanks and pray for good fortune.

THE POTLATCH

American Indians in the Northwest hold another traditional celebration—the potlatch. Long ago, wealthy tribal leaders hosted these events. The hosts gave away food and gifts to their guests. Through potlatches, leaders helped poorer members of their tribe.

In modern times, host families hold potlatches to observe important events in their lives. Potlatches may celebrate a wedding, a birthday, or an anniversary. They may take place over several days. Hosts try hard to impress their guests with gifts. These are often practical items, such as towels or dishes. Honored guests and elders, however, may receive handmade baskets, blankets, or other expensive presents. A family sometimes saves for years to have enough money to hold a successful potlatch.

POWWOWS

Not all American Indian celebrations are traditional. In fact, the most popular get-togethers—powwows—are modern events. At these social gatherings, people come together to enjoy music, dancing, and food. Powwows can be small gatherings at which friends and family visit with one another for a few hours. But some powwows are major

Dancers enter the arena during the Gathering of Nations in Albuquerque, New Mexico, in 2006. A yearly event, this powwow is the largest in North America.

events. They may last for days and attract thousands of American Indians from many different tribes. A few are open to non-Indians.

The biggest powwow in North America is the Gathering of Nations. This celebration has been held in Albuquerque, New Mexico, every year since 1983. It is a showcase for more than three thousand dancers and singers from about five hundred tribes. The powwow has thirty-two dancing competitions as well as a pageant for Miss Indian World. The event also features a huge Indian Traders Market, where American Indian artisans sell their jewelry, baskets, and other handicrafts. In addition, food booths offer visitors traditional dishes and powwow favorites, such as buffalo burgers, acorn soup, and fried corn on the cob.

Fancy Dancing

One of the high points of any powwow is the fancy dancing. Fancy dancing is a spirited form of dance *(see photo on page 48)*. It is known for its intense shaking and fast footwork. Young men usually perform fancy dancing. Sometimes they improvise flashy moves. In the middle of the dance, they may do the splits or a backflip.

Fancy dancing was developed by American Indians living on reservations in the 1920s. It was meant to be a showstopper at performances for non-Indian tourists. The clothing worn by fancy dancers is just as showy as their movements. Bright and big, the outfits are often adorned with giant bustles of brilliantly colored feathers.

RETHINKING COLUMBUS DAY AND THANKSGIVING

American Indians enjoy most of the holidays celebrated in the United States. They exchange gifts on Valentine's Day. They honor war veterans on Veterans Day. They go to barbecues and watch fireworks on Independence Day. But many American Indians have mixed feelings about two big holidays—Columbus Day and Thanksgiving.

Columbus Day commemorates the arrival of Italian explorer Christopher Columbus in North America in 1492. For many American Indians, the event is nothing to celebrate. They view the arrival of Europeans as a disaster for Indian peoples. In their eyes, Columbus's voyage marked the beginning of centuries of war and disease, which led to the complete destruction of many tribes.

For this reason, some American Indians hold protests at

Columbus Day festivities. They do not celebrate Columbus Day as a holiday. They instead observe it as a National Day of Mourning.

Most traditional American Indian cultures held thanksgiving ceremonies. Modern Indian peoples also believe in setting aside time to give thanks. Many American Indians say prayers of thanksgiving often—sometimes even daily.

The American Thanksgiving holiday, however, celebrates a specific event—a feast attended by Wampanoag Indians and English Pilgrims of the Plymouth colony in present-day Massachusetts in 1621. The friendship between the Wampanoags and the English did not last long. They were soon in a deadly war, as the English began taking over the Wampanoags' territory. Some American Indians feel the uplifting tale of the first Thanksgiving gives a false impression of history. It puts a pretty face on the ugly story of American Indians and the English in early America.

CELEBRATING AMERICAN INDIAN HERITAGE

In recent years, Americans have begun to observe several new celebrations of American Indian life and culture. Every year since 1994, the federal government has named November National American Indian and Alaska Native Heritage Month.

This American Indian woman holds a protest sign at a rally in Michigan on Columbus Day.

AMERICA WAS ALREADY DISCOVERED!

www.usatoday.com

News

SECTION A

November 25, 1998

From the Pages of USA TODAY

At Plymouth, equal time for Indians
March OK'd after 1997's troubles

The annual Pilgrim Progress march of locals dressed as Pilgrims will once again wind through town Thursday. But this year, in the birthplace of Thanksgiving, the Indians get equal time. Not everyone is thankful.

As the result of a nasty fracas [conflict] between police and protesters last year, the town has given its nervous blessing to an anticipated gathering of 1,500 demonstrators, expected to range from local Wampanoag Indians to gay rights activists.

Police who will oversee the National Day of Mourning march are angry that charges against last year's protesters were dropped. [But] the Indians are celebrating.

"After three decades of our trying to get the truth out, Plymouth has acknowledged our truth is as valid as theirs," says Moonanum Roland James, a Wampanoag Indian and retired Navy musician who leads the United American Indians group.

The modern war between the Indians and Plymouth began in 1970 when James' father, Wamsutta Frank James, was asked to speak at the 350th anniversary of the Plymouth Rock landing, to promote the vision of brotherhood of Pilgrim and Indian.

But the elder James' proposed speech offered a darker view. "We, the Wampanoag, welcomed you, the white man, with open arms, little knowing that it was the beginning of the end," James' father planned to say, after reciting a [list] of massacres and broken treaties.

His invitation was withdrawn when he refused suggested revisions, and the [conflict that followed] led to what Indians called the National Day of Mourning. For the past 27 Thanksgivings, a few hundred protesters gathered at noon on Cole's Hill overlooking Plymouth Rock to decry treatment of Native Americans.

For Caroline Kardell, the local Mayflower Society's historian-general, there is enough town history to accommodate all. The enthusiastic, gray-haired woman says Pilgrim and Indian did get along until Puritans from the Massachusetts Bay colony began to crowd in and push Indians out.

For the future, Kardell sees hope for unifying the different views of the past.

"The Indians have traditionally been invisible except for Thanksgiving," she says. "This could end up being a good thing for the cause of Indian identity."

—*Fred Bayles*

Museums and schools across the United States hold special programs and events. They educate the public about the history and traditions of American Indians and Alaska's native peoples.

Two states also celebrate Native American Day. South Dakota was the first to do so. Since 1990 Native American Day has been a state holiday observed on October 12, the traditional date for Columbus Day. An American Indian-run newspaper, *Indian Country Today* (formerly the *Lakota Times*), had pushed for the holiday. The paper's campaign convinced the state government to make Native American Day a reality.

California lawmakers followed South Dakota's example in 1998. In California, Native American Day is observed on the fourth Friday of every September. California State University at San Bernardino stages a big exhibition. There, people can see American Indian art, listen to American Indian music, and snack on delicious American Indian foods.

In 2008, for the first time, the U.S. Congress named the day after Thanksgiving as a national Native American Heritage Day. Seven years before, Frank Suniga, a Mescalero Apache living in Oregon, first came up with the idea. He asked for the support of the Affiliated Tribes of Northwest Indians. That organization got the National Congress of American Indians and other Indian groups on board. They put pressure on Congress to pass a law designating a national day to celebrate tribal heritage. The law set aside the day for only that one year, however. American Indian groups hope to persuade Congress to make it an annual event.

CHAPTER 6:

NATIVE FOODS

Imagine a huge buffet table covered with delicious dishes. Looking at all the selections, you start planning your meal. You might start with a bowl of rich seafood chowder or hearty stew. For your main dish, you may have a slice of roast turkey, a piece of grilled salmon, or maybe a buffalo steak. But you also want to leave some room to sample the tasty sides. You are especially tempted by the roasted corn on the cob, the steaming wild rice, the toasty squares of corn bread, and the bean-and-corn succotash. After all that food, you think a light dessert would hit

For centuries, many American Indians have grown corn, beans, and squash. These vegetables could be stored to provide people with food long after they were first harvested.

the spot. You decide to have a fruit salad made from fresh berries. There are dozens of varieties—from strawberries to blackberries to chokeberries.

All the dishes on this imaginary buffet have something in common. They are all made from the enormous variety of foods that Indian peoples enjoyed before the arrival of non-Indians in North America. Many of these foods have become familiar to all Americans.

A WORLD OF VARIETY

The foods American Indians ate over the centuries depended on where they lived. In the Northeast, for instance, men hunted small animals and birds and large game, such as deer. They also fished in the area's many rivers and lakes. Women added to the food stores by tending gardens. During the fall, the harvest gave these American Indians the most important staples of their diet—corn, beans, and squash. The Iroquois paid tribute to these crops by calling them the Three Sisters.

These crops were also important to American Indians in the Southwest. The Navajos, for example, sang a planting song about how the spirits of corn, beans, and squash were friends. After non-Indians introduced sheep to North America, the Navajos became skilled herders. Lamb and mutton then also became staples of their diet.

In the Northwest, American Indians found a wealth of food in the ocean and rivers. Along beaches, they collected oysters and mussels. Occasionally, they feasted on whales that washed ashore. But their most important food was salmon. During the annual salmon runs, American Indian fishers always came away with an impressive catch. Northwestern

This painting from the mid-1800s shows American Indians fishing for salmon at Kettle Falls on the Columbia River in Washington.

American Indians developed many ways to dry and preserve fish. As a result, they had plenty of food all year round.

Some American Indian peoples got much of their nutrition from a single food that grew wild in their lands. The Chumash of present-day California, for example, feasted on acorns. The Nez Percé of modern-day Idaho relied on wild camas, a type of lily plant with an edible root. The Ojibwe of the Great Lakes region enjoyed many dishes made from wild rice that grows in wetlands.

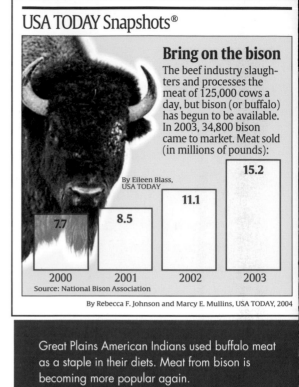

USA TODAY Snapshots®

Bring on the bison

The beef industry slaughters and processes the meat of 125,000 cows a day, but bison (or buffalo) has begun to be available. In 2003, 34,800 bison came to market. Meat sold (in millions of pounds):

By Eileen Blass, USA TODAY

2000	2001	2002	2003
7.7	8.5	11.1	15.2

Source: National Bison Association

By Rebecca F. Johnson and Marcy E. Mullins, USA TODAY, 2004

Great Plains American Indians used buffalo meat as a staple in their diets. Meat from bison is becoming more popular again.

In the mid-1700s, tribes in the Great Plains first obtained horses, which the Spanish had brought to North America in the 1500s. On horseback, American Indians of the Plains began to hunt great herds of buffalo. Buffalo meat quickly became a large part of their diets. Buffalo also provided other necessities. Buffalo skins, for example, were made into clothes and tipis. Plains Indians also crafted tools from buffalo bones and made candles and soap from buffalo fat. They burned buffalo manure as a fuel.

CHANGING FOOD TRADITIONS

Over time, as non-Indians began to take over the Indians' lands, many American Indians lost their traditional hunting and fishing grounds.

Pumpkin Seeds

Americans Indians traditionally ate the seeds of pumpkins. Pumpkin seeds are not only nutritious. When toasted, they also have a sweet, nutty flavor. Next Halloween, be sure to save the seeds from your jack-o'-lantern. You can use your microwave to make them into a tasty American Indian-style treat.

INGREDIENTS
fresh pumpkin seeds
vegetable oil
salt

PREPARATION

1. Rinse pumpkin seeds to remove any pulp.

2. Pat them down with paper towels, and spread them on a cookie sheet. Let them dry overnight.

3. Place seeds in a single layer on a glass baking dish. Sprinkle with a little oil and salt. Use your hands to toss the seeds, making sure all are coated with oil.

4. Microwave for 2 minutes on high, and then stir the seeds. Microwave for 1 minute more and stir, repeating this step until the seeds are a light brown color. Expect a total cooking time of about 5 to 8 minutes.

5. Let the seeds cool slightly before serving. Store the leftovers in an airtight container or plastic bag.

They also were barred from areas where nutritious wild plants grew. In time, most American Indians no longer had access to many of the foods they had depended on for centuries.

The situation worsened in the 1800s. At that time, the U.S. government began forcing American Indians onto reservations. These areas were usually smaller than their traditional territories. Sometimes reservations were hundreds of miles away from where a tribe had originally lived.

On reservations, American Indians had to rely on food rations (supplies) from the U.S. government. The rations were non-Indian foodstuffs unfamiliar to many Indian peoples. Rations usually included white flour, sugar, and lard.

During this time, government officials tried to force American Indians to give up their historic customs. At government-run schools, American Indian students were told that Indian ways were bad and non-Indian ways were good. As a result, young American Indians began rejecting Indian foods. Many never learned to cook the recipes of their parents and grandparents. By the late 1900s, most American Indian people regularly ate few, if any, traditional dishes.

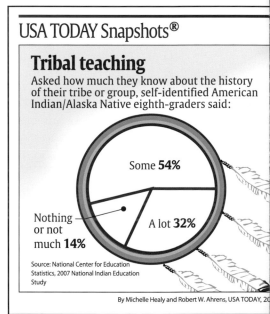

USA TODAY Snapshots®

Tribal teaching

Asked how much they know about the history of their tribe or group, self-identified American Indian/Alaska Native eighth-graders said:

Some **54%**

A lot **32%**

Nothing or not much **14%**

Source: National Center for Education Statistics, 2007 National Indian Education Study

By Michelle Healy and Robert W. Ahrens, USA TODAY, 20

Many tribal teachings were lost when American Indians were forced to attend government-run schools. But recent efforts to reintroduce traditional teachings mean that more young American Indians are learning about their culture.

www.usatoday.com

USA TODAY

News

SECTION A

October 4, 1999

From the Pages of USA TODAY

Way of life could fade with whale population

For centuries, Indians from [the] village [of Tyonek, Alaska] have ventured into the waters of Cook Inlet to kill beluga whales. They hunted them for food and to reaffirm ancient cultural traditions.

Now the belugas are disappearing, and villagers see an irreplaceable piece of their heritage going with them. A ban on hunting this year might be extended indefinitely.

"It could mean the younger generation will never know... the way we used to live," says Peter Merryman, chief of Tyonek's Athabaskan tribe.

Most whale hunting is banned by international treaty, but Native Alaskans are allowed to harvest the whales for subsistence [food] under an exemption in the Marine Mammal Protection Act.

Historically, the inlet sustains about 1,000 belugas, but the population has dwindled to 350, according to counts this year. Some Native Alaskans believe the number is even smaller.

The people of Tyonek take no more than two or three whales a year for subsistence. But hunters from other regions, many of whom left their villages for permanent jobs in Anchorage, have been taking 50 or more. Conservationists say these hunters have been selling muktuk—the skin and thin layer of blubber underneath that's prized by Native Alaskans—for profit.

The urban hunters deny that they're harvesting belugas for [money]. They say they're merely providing muktuk to Native Alaskans who cannot hunt and who have no other access to an important traditional food.

In May, Sen. Ted Stevens, R[epublican]-Alaska, pushed a hunting ban through Congress after Tyonek's tribal government and the urban hunters failed to negotiate a plan to control hunting. The urban hunters eventually agreed to stop hunting until the whales make a comeback. Tyonek's request to take two whales this summer was denied.

[Meanwhile], many of the tourists who clamber off the tour buses at Beluga Point in the upper inlet south of Anchorage will be disappointed. Where dozens of belugas could often be seen in the past, now only a few whales show up from time to time. And the hunters in Tyonek can only hope their village elders will live long enough to pass on their knowledge if hunting is ever allowed again.

—*John Ritter*

FAVORITE AMERICAN INDIAN DISHES

In the twenty-first century, American Indians eat many of the same foods as other Americans do. At home they might have hot dogs, hamburgers, or macaroni and cheese. When they go out to eat, they might stop off for fast food or go to a restaurant serving popular dishes of another American ethnic group, such as Italian American pasta or Japanese American sushi. Even when American Indians eat roast turkey or succotash, they, like other Americans, do not likely think of these as Indian foods. These have been part of the standard American diet for so long that they have largely lost their association with Indian cultures.

Even so, contemporary American Indians do enjoy some uniquely Indian dishes. For very traditional families, these might be part of everyday meals. But most American Indians eat these foods only on special occasions or during festivals or ceremonies.

Many of these dishes are native to southwestern groups. Unlike most other American Indian peoples, some southwestern Indians, such as the Navajo people and the Pueblo tribes, were able to stay on their traditional homelands. As a result, fewer of their old ways were lost. Visitors to the Navajo reservation are likely to be invited for a meal of mutton stew, which remains a favorite food of the Navajos. The Hopi and the Zuni Pueblos still cook piki. This thin bread is made from blue corn they grow themselves.

Groups in other areas have also held on to a few dishes that remind them of their heritage. Several Great Lakes tribes still gather wild rice in the late summer. On the Plains, American Indians still make *wojape*—a pudding of mashed berries. They also enjoy pemmican, a snack made from dried buffalo meat mixed with lard and berries. The American Indians of the Northwest continue to eat fish and seafood. Halibut and salmon are particularly popular.

Pemmican

While traveling, American Indians of the Plains relied on pemmican. This portable food was made from dried meat, fat, and berries. Sometimes crushed nuts were added. This American Indian version of trail mix was nutritious and high in calories. It also took a long time to spoil. As long as pemmican was kept dry, it was edible for years.

This modern recipe for pemmican leaves out the meat and fat. But true to the traditional American Indian food, the recipe is flexible. Like pemmican makers of the past, feel free to use whatever dried fruits and nuts you have on hand.

INGREDIENTS

handful of dried fruits (such as cranberries, cherries, and raisins)
handful of nuts
honey

PREPARATION

1. Blend the fruits and nuts in a food processor. Place the mixture in a large bowl.

2. Slowly drizzle honey into the bowl. Add only the amount needed to make the fruit-and-nut mixture bind together.

3. Place a few spoonfuls of the mixture onto a sheet of wax paper. Mold the mixture in the sheet so it is the size and shape of a candy bar. Wrap the paper tightly around the bar, and place it in the refrigerator. Repeat this step until all of the mixture has been made into bars.

4. Refrigerate the bars for about an hour, or until they are firm. Serve as a snack.

PAN-INDIAN FOODS

Contemporary American Indians also enjoy pan-Indian foods. These dishes are not part of any one tribal tradition. American Indians often enjoy these foods at powwows, where they are sold at food booths.

One popular powwow food is fry bread. Fry bread is made from white flour, water, baking powder, and salt. These ingredients are mixed together to make a dough. Balls of dough are then deep fried in lard or oil until they are puffed up and crispy on the outside. Fry bread is often topped with powdered sugar or honey to make a sweet snack. For a more substantial meal, fry bread is cupped like a taco shell and filled with meat, cheese, chilies, tomatoes, and lettuce.

REVIVING OLD FOODS

In recent years, many tribal groups have tried to revive forgotten food traditions. In this way, some of these groups hope to preserve their tribe's culture and heritage. For instance, the White Earth Land Recovery Project—an Ojibwe group dedicated to buying back Ojibwe land and promoting Ojibwe culture—started the Mino-Miijim (Good Food) Program to provide tribespeople with traditional foods. As the organization explains, "Our ancestors understood the importance of . . . eating in harmony with the earth. That is why so many stories deal with the sacred nature of our traditional foods. Eating these traditional foods re-connects us with the stories and traditions of our people."

Other groups want to work for better health among American Indian peoples. One is the Tohono O'odhams of Arizona. About half of all Tohono O'odhams are diabetic. They have the highest rate of diabetes among any group of people in the world.

USA TODAY
CULTURAL MOSAIC

The Fry Bread Controversy

Each year hundreds of American Indian festivals take place across the United States. Nearly all of them have one thing in common: the tasty treat called fry bread is likely to be for sale. Many American Indians love this snack. But even though it is popular, fry bread is not truly an American Indian dish. It dates from the 1800s—a time during which many tribes were forced onto reservations. Reservation residents were often close to starvation. For food, they had to rely on government rations of non-Indian foods, such as lard and flour. Turning these ingredients into fried bread made sense. It may not have been nutritious, but it tasted good—and, more important to very hungry people, it had a lot of calories.

Recently, fry bread has become a controversial part of American Indian life. For many American Indians, fry bread is a fun, festive treat. But for some, it is a symbol of the reservation system that oppressed Indian peoples. Perhaps even worse, it is a cause of obesity—a health problem that affects many American Indian communities.

In January 2005, writer and activist Suzan Shown Harjo took a stand against fry bread. In a column published in the newspaper *Indian Country Today*, she declared that she was giving up fry bread as her New Year's resolution. She wrote, "Frybread is [symbolic] of the long trails from home and freedom to confinement and rations. It's the connecting dot between healthy children and obesity . . . diabetes [a disease sometimes associated with obesity], . . . and slow death." She advised American Indian cooks to do the same and start making truly traditional Indian breads and foods full of healthful ingredients. Harjo told anyone who prepared these foods for their families to "prepare to see some smiles."

The Tohono O'odhams decided that the modern American diet was making them overweight and ill. So the tribe is promoting a traditional diet as a way of losing weight and managing or preventing diabetes. Traditional foods such as mesquite beans, cholla buds, and chia seeds might actually slow sugar absorption in diabetics, who have an abnormally high level of blood sugar.

Other tribes have started programs designed to preserve traditional foods and farming methods for future generations. Southwestern American Indians, with the help of students at the University of Arizona, are collecting seeds from old varieties of native crops. They then provide the seeds free to American Indian farmers.

One of the most ambitious projects is the InterTribal Bison Cooperative. It was established in 1990. By the late 1800s, white hunters had killed so many Great Plains buffalo that they were nearly extinct. The bison cooperative wants to restore the great herds "to preserve our historical, cultural, traditional, and spiritual relationship for future generations."

AMERICAN INDIAN FOOD AND WORLD CUISINE

American Indians are not the only people interested in preserving their food traditions. Many non-Indians want to know more about Indians' contribution to world cuisine. Several annual festivals teach both Indians and non-Indians about the subject. One of the biggest is the Celebration of Basketweaving and Native Foods Festival held at the Heard Museum in Phoenix, Arizona, every December. At this event, people can watch demonstrations of American Indian cooks making piki bread, roasting salmon, and parching corn.

Chef Loretta Barrett Oden also wants to educate all Americans about American Indian foods and cooking. A member of the

Patrons line up for food at Mitsitam Café at the National Museum of the American Indian in Washington, D.C. The restaurant serves American Indian-style food.

Potawatomi tribe, she hosts *Seasoned with Spirit: A Native Chef's Journey with Loretta Barrett Oden*. The thirteen-part television series examines American Indian food traditions throughout the United States.

In the nation's capital, anyone interested in sampling American Indian cuisine can visit the Mitsitam Café. The restaurant is in the National Museum of the American Indian in Washington, D.C. The menu offers a modern take on traditional American Indian cooking.

According to scholar Gary Nabhan, "The Mitsitam Café gives more than a hundred thousand Americans a gift every year. They're bringing us as close as possible to the first textures and flavors of America." In this way, the restaurant provides guests with a valuable lesson about American Indian culture while exciting their taste buds. As Nabhan points out, "We don't just learn with our heads; we learn with our palates, too."

FAMOUS AMERICAN INDIANS

Adam Beach

(b. 1972) Ojibwe actor Adam Beach is one of the hottest American Indian stars in film. Born on the Dog Creek Reserve near Ashern, Manitoba, Canada, Beach discovered acting in high school drama class. Deciding to make it his career, he quickly landed roles on several Canadian television series. Beach attracted the attention of Hollywood after starring in the movie *Smoke Signals* (1998). He then played the lead in *Windtalkers* (2002), for which he spent months studying the Navajo language. Beach has since appeared in the films *Skinwalkers* (2002) and *Flags of Our Fathers* (2006). He has also become a fixture on television. In 2007 alone, he joined the cast of *Law & Order: Special Victims Unit* and starred in the television movie *Bury My Heart at Wounded Knee*.

Winona LaDuke

(b. 1959) American Indian activist Winona LaDuke was born in Los Angeles, California. An Ojibwe, she frequently visited the White Earth Indian Reservation in Minnesota to learn more about her heritage. After graduating from Harvard University in Cambridge, Massachusetts, LaDuke moved to White Earth, determined to help the people of this poor reservation community. LaDuke founded the White Earth Land Recovery Project with the goal of buying back land that the U.S. government illegally seized from the Ojibwe people. A strong environmentalist, LaDuke is also involved with the Green Party (a political group that supports environmental causes). In the 1996 and 2000 national elections, she was the party's vice-presidential candidate, running with presidential candidate Ralph Nader.

Wilma Mankiller

(b. 1945) Wilma Mankiller was the first woman elected to lead a major American Indian tribe. She was born in the Cherokee Nation in Oklahoma and moved to California as a girl. There she became involved in a 1969 protest on Alcatraz, an island off the coast of San Francisco, in which American Indians of many tribes came together to demand cultural respect and self-determination (the right of American Indian communities to take care of themselves). In 1977 Mankiller returned to Oklahoma and took a job as a community organizer with the Cherokee government. Her work so impressed Ross Swimmer, a candidate for the Cherokees' principal chief, that he asked her to join his ticket as a deputy chief candidate. She was elected in 1983. After Swimmer

USA TODAY.
CULTURAL MOSAIC

took a job with the U.S. government, Mankiller became principal chief two years later. She proved to be a popular leader and was reelected twice. Mankiller retired from politics in 1995. She continues to lecture and teach college classes on issues facing American Indians.

Billy Mills

(b. 1938) Raised on a reservation in South Dakota, Lakota Sioux runner Billy Mills went to college on a track scholarship. After serving in the U.S. Marine Corps, he competed in many international racing competitions. At the 1964 Olympics in Tokyo, Japan, Mills stunned the crowd as he came from behind to win a gold medal in the 10,000-meter race. He set a new Olympic record and became the only American ever to win that event. Mills's accomplishment inspired the 1983 movie *Running Brave.* He currently works as an advocate for young American Indians in need through his charity, Running Strong for American Indian Youth.

N. Scott Momaday

(b. 1934) Kiowa writer N. Scott Momaday won the Pulitzer Prize in 1969 for his novel *House Made of Dawn.* Raised in the Southwest, Momaday was inspired as a boy by his father, Al, who was a visual artist. Momaday began writing poetry and taught literature at several schools. At the University of California–Berkeley, he established one of the first American Indian literature programs. Following the success of *House Made of Dawn*, Momaday wrote several more novels and volumes of poetry. In the 1970s, Momaday also took up drawing and painting. His artwork has been exhibited across the United States.

Lori Piestewa

(1979–2003) Lori Piestewa was the first American Indian woman soldier serving in the U.S. Army to be killed in combat. Of Hopi descent, she was raised in Tuba City, Arizona, on the Navajo Indian Reservation. Following in the footsteps of her father and grandfather, Piestewa joined the U.S. Army in 2001. Two years later, she took part in the U.S. invasion of Iraq. On the third day of the Iraq war, she was driving a Humvee in a convoy headed for Baghdad, the capital of Iraq. After the convoy took a wrong turn, it was attacked by the Iraqi Army. Her vehicle crashed, and she was taken as a prisoner of war. In an Iraqi hospital, Piestewa died of her injuries. The army later awarded Piestewa the Purple Heart. Arizona honors her memory with an annual athletic competition called the Lori Piestewa National Native American Games.

EXPLORE YOUR HERITAGE

Where did your family come from? Who are your relatives, and where do they live? Were they born in the United States? If not, when and why did they come here? Where did you get your family name? Is it German? Puerto Rican? Vietnamese? Something else? If you are adopted, what is your adoptive family's story?

By searching for the answers to these questions, you can begin to discover your family's history. And if your family history is hard to trace, team up with a friend to share ideas or to learn more about that person's family history.

Where to Start

Start with what you know. In a notebook or on your family's computer, write down the full names of the relatives you know about and anything you know about them—where they lived, what they liked to do as children, any awards or honors they earned, and so on.

Next, gather some primary sources. Primary sources are the records and observations of eyewitnesses to events. They include diaries; letters; autobiographies; speeches; newspapers; birth, marriage, and death records; photographs; and ship records. The best primary resources about your family may be in family scrapbooks or files in your home or in your relatives' homes. You may also find some interesting material in libraries, archives, historical societies, and museums. These organizations often have primary sources available online.

The Next Steps

After taking notes and gathering primary sources, think about what facts and details you are missing. You can then prepare to interview your relatives to see if they can fill in these gaps. First, write down any questions that you would like to ask them about their lives. Then ask your relatives if they would mind being interviewed. Don't be upset if they say no. Understand that some people do not like to talk about their pasts.

Also, consider interviewing family friends. They can often provide interesting stories and details about your relatives. They might have photographs too.

Family Interviews

When you are ready for an interview, gather your questions, a notepad, a tape recorder or camcorder, and any other materials you might need. Consider showing your interview subjects a photograph or a timetable of important events at the start of your interview. These items can help jog the memory of your subjects and get them talking. You might also bring U.S. and world maps to an interview. Ask your subjects to label the places they have lived.

Remember that people's memories aren't always accurate. Sometimes they forget information and confuse dates. You might want to take a trip to the library or look online to check dates and other facts.

Get Organized!

When you finish your interviews and research, you are ready to organize your information. There are many ways of doing this. You can write a history of your entire family or individual biographies of your relatives. You can create a timeline going back to your earliest known ancestors. You can make a family tree—a diagram or chart that shows how people in your family are related to one another.

If you have collected a lot of photographs, consider compiling a photo album or scrapbook that tells your family history. Or if you used a camcorder to record your interviews, you might even want to make a movie.

However you put together your family history, be sure to share it! Your relatives will want to see all the information you found. You might want to create a website or blog so that other people can learn about your family. Whatever you choose to do, you'll end up with something your family will appreciate for years to come.

AMERICAN INDIAN SNAPSHOT

This chart shows a statistical snapshot of the five largest American Indian groups living in the United States. It looks at how many American Indians from each group are living in the country and which states have the greatest populations. All figures are based on individuals claiming full or partial ancestry in the designated American Indian group in the 2000 U.S. Census. In this census, about four million Americans said they were at least part American Indian or Alaskan Native.

For more information on American Indian and Alaskan Native populations, see http://www.census.gov/prod/2007pubs/acs-07.pdf.

AMERICAN INDIAN GROUP	TOTAL U.S. POPULATION	FIVE TOP STATES OF RESIDENCE
Cherokee	729,533	Oklahoma: 156,831 California: 97,838 Texas: 45,151 Florida: 29,602 Ohio: 25,171
Navajo	298,197	Arizona: 131,166 New Mexico: 106,807 Utah: 16,445 Colorado: 6,858 Nevada: 1,860
Choctaw	158,774	Oklahoma: 65,145 Texas: 18,780 Mississippi: 7,684 Louisiana: 4,653 Arkansas: 3,560
Sioux	153,360	South Dakota: 55,644 North Dakota: 9,215 Minnesota: 7,541 Montana: 5,793 Nebraska: 5,344
Chippewa	149,669	Minnesota: 39,910 Michigan: 32,267 Wisconsin: 15,560 North Dakota: 14,803 California: 7,166

GLOSSARY

fancy dancing: a style of modern powwow dancing with fast, athletic movements

fry bread: a popular contemporary American Indian food made from a white flour dough fried in lard or oil

lacrosse: a modern sport similar to ancient American Indian ball games, in which players use a netted racket to throw a ball into a goal

missionary: someone who is sent by a church or religious group to teach that group's faith to others

Native American Church: a religion dating from the late 1800s that combines elements of traditional American Indian spiritual beliefs and Christianity

pan-Indian: relating to American Indians of many different tribes

pemmican: a mixture of dried buffalo meat, lard, and berries that American Indians of the Plains often ate while traveling

peyote: part of a mescal cactus that is eaten during religious ceremonies by members of the Native American Church

potlatch: a celebration held by American Indians of the Pacific Northwest in which a host family holds a feast and gives gifts to guests

powwow: an American Indian social event in which people gather to enjoy music, dancing, and foods

rations: food supplies that the U.S. government gave to American Indians living on reservations. Rations usually included white flour, sugar, and lard.

reservation: a tract of land set aside by the U.S. government for the use of a specific American Indian group. The first reservation was established in 1638. At the beginning of the twenty-first century, there were about three hundred reservations in the United States.

traditional: related to historic customs

tribe: a group of people who share the same ancestors, cultural and religious customs, laws, and language

vision quest: a ceremony in which a youth of about the age of twelve, after consulting with elders, goes into the wilderness alone to experience the spirit world

Western: a movie set in the American West in the late 1800s, often with American Indian peoples portrayed as villains

SOURCE NOTES

16 Helen Cedar Tree, quoted in Dan Frosch, "Its Native Tongue Facing Extinction, Arapaho Tribe Teaches the Young," *New York Times*, October 17, 2008.

17 Ryan Wilson, quoted in Dan Frosch, "Its Native Tongue Facing Extinction, Arapaho Tribe Teaches the Young," *New York Times*, October 17, 2008.

33 Bob Bernotas, *Jim Thorpe* (New York: Chelsea House Publishers, 1992), 19.

34 Maurice Smith, quoted in Greg Boeck, "The Native American Barrier," *USA Today*, February 22, 2007, C1.

47 National Museum of the American Indian, *Do All Indians Live in Tipis?: Questions & Answers from the National Museum of the American Indian* (New York: Collins, 2007), 115.

51 Alfred Gibson, quoted in Jennifer Miller, "Federal Government Taps Ancient Healing Methods to Treat Native American Soldiers," *Christian Science Monitor*, September 13, 2007.

66 White Earth Land Recovery Project, "Mino-Miijim (Good Food) Program," *White Earth Land Recovery Project & Native Harvest Online Catalog*, 2008, http://nativeharvest.com/node/2 (November 20, 2008).

67 Suzan Shown Harjo, "My New Year's Resolution: No More Fat 'Indian' Food," *Indian Country Today*, January 20, 2005.

68 "Introduction," InterTribal Bison Cooperative, 2009, http://www.itbcbison.com/index.php (November 20, 2008).

69 Gary Nabhan, quoted in Gabriella Boston, "American Indian Variations at Café," *Washington Times*, July 30, 2008, B01.

SELECTED BIBLIOGRAPHY

Berzok, Linda Murray. *American Indian Food*. Westport, CT: Greenwood Press, 2005.
This book provides an in-depth history of American Indian foods and the traditions associated with them.

Davis, Mary B., ed. *Native America in the Twentieth Century: An Encyclopedia*. New York: Garland Publishing, 1996.
Through hundreds of articles, this encyclopedia focuses on contemporary American Indian issues and federal policies relating to American Indians.

Feest, Christian F. *Native Arts of North America*. Rev. ed. New York: Thames and Hudson, 1992.
This classic work discusses the art and artistic traditions of American Indians throughout North America.

Hirshfelder, Arlene, Paulette Molin, and Walter R. Echo-Hawk. *The Encyclopedia of Native American Religions*. Rev. ed. New York: Facts on File, 1999.
This reference work provides a comprehensive account of the spiritual traditions, practices, and beliefs of North America's native peoples.

Hoxie, Frederick E., ed. *Encyclopedia of North American Indians*. Boston: Houghton Mifflin Company, 1996.
An excellent reference, this encyclopedia features many articles written by American Indian scholars.

King, C. Richard, ed. *Native Athletes in Sport and Society: A Reader*. Lincoln: University of Nebraska Press, 2005.
A collection of essays, this reader explores the role sports have played in American Indian life.

Ruoff, A. LaVonne Brown. *Literatures of the American Indian*. New York: Chelsea House Publishers, 1991.
This book provides a short yet thorough introduction of the oral and written literatures of American Indians.

Waldman, Carl. *Atlas of the North American Indian*. 3rd ed. New York: Facts on File, 2009.
Combining many maps with a running narrative, this atlas offers an overview of American Indian history and culture.

FURTHER READING AND WEBSITES

Alexie, Sherman. *The Absolutely True Diary of a Part-Time Indian*. New York: Little, Brown, 2007.
Sherman's popular fictional novel for young adults follows fourteen-year-old Arnold Spirit Jr. as he encounters challenges in school and at home on the Spokane Indian Reservation.

Capaldi, Gina. *A Boy Named Beckoning: The True Story of Dr. Carlos Montezuma, Native American Hero*. Minneapolis: Carolrhoda Books, 2008.
This title tells the incredible life story of an American Indian boy named Wassaja, or "Beckoning," who overcomes enormous hardships to become a doctor and an American Indian rights activist.

Golus, Carrie. *Jim Thorpe*. Minneapolis: Twenty-First Century Books, 2008.
Learn more about American Indian Olympian Jim Thorpe in this engaging selection.

Indian Country Today
http://www.indiancountrytoday.com
Operated by the Oneida Indian Nation, *Indian Country Today* is a weekly newspaper covering stories from American Indian communities across the United States.

Murdoch, David S. *North American Indian*. New York: DK, 2005.
This title features numerous full-color photos and a wealth of interesting information about North America's native peoples.

National Museum of the American Indian
http://www.nmai.si.edu
The official site of the National Museum of the American Indian in Washington, D.C., features online exhibitions, many of which include artwork and other objects from the museum's vast collection.

National Museum of the American Indian. *Do All Indians Live in Tipis?: Questions and Answers from the National Museum of the American Indian*. New York: HarperCollins, 2007.
This book provides useful answers to questions about American Indians while breaking common stereotypes.

Native Youth Magazine
http://www.nativeyouthmagazine.com
This site is an online magazine for American Indian young people from across the United States and Canada.

Sonneborn, Liz. *Chronology of American Indian History*. Rev. ed. New York: Facts on File, 2007.
A timeline of American Indian life in North America, this title offers information on American Indian origins, culture, reservations, and much more.

INDEX

PHOTO ACKNOWLEDGMENTS

The images in this book are used with the permission of: © MPI/Hulton Archive/ Getty Images, pp. 3 (top), 30, 59; Library of Congress, pp. 3 (second from top, LC-USZ62-122858), 8 (LC-USZ62-122858), 43 (LC-USZ62-98166); REUTERS/Paul Darrow, pp. 3 (center), 31; © Marilyn Angel Wynn/Nativestock.com, pp. 3 (third from top, third from bottom), 19, 41, 67; © Anders Ryman/CORBIS, pp. 3 (second from bottom), 50; © Marilyn Angel Wynn/Nativestock.com/Getty Images, pp. 3 (bottom), 48, 58; © Bettmann/CORBIS, p. 4; © Michael Madrid/USA TODAY, p. 5; The Granger Collection, New York, p. 6; © Leonard McCombe/Time & Life Pictures/Getty Images, p. 7; © North Wind Picture Archives, p. 9; © Ulf Andersen/Getty Images, pp. 10, 14, 71 (center); © Tim Dillon/USA TODAY, p. 12; Photo by Tony Celentano, Courtesy of Ofelia Zepeda, p. 13; AP Photo/Don Ryan, p. 17; © Kathleen Greeson/USA TODAY, p. 18; © Emilie Sommer/USA TODAY, p. 20; © Stephen Shugerman/Getty Images, pp. 21, 70 (bottom); © The Bridgeman Art Library/Getty Images, p. 23; © Evan Eile/USA TODAY, p. 25; © Orion Pictures/Courtesy: Everett Collection, p. 27; © Andy Lyons/Getty Images, p. 32; © Topical Press Agency/Hulton Archive/Getty Images, p. 33; © Eileen Blass/USA TODAY, p. 34; © Tom Bean/CORBIS, p. 38; Courtesy of SuAnne Big Crow Boys and Girls Club, p. 39; © Sylvain Grandadam/The Image Bank/Getty Images, p. 40; AP Photo/Fort Worth Star-Telegram, Joyce Marshall, p. 44; © Jeff Smith/Alamy, p. 45; The Art Archive/Chandler-Pohrt Collection, Gift of Mr and Mrs Richard A Pohrt/Buffalo Bill Historical Center, Cody, Wyoming/NA.502.183 A-B, p. 46; © Michael Greenlar/The Image Works, p. 49; © Ed Kashi/CORBIS, p. 51; AP Photo/The New Mexican, Luis Sanchez Saturno, p. 53; © Jim West/Alamy, p. 55; © iStockphoto.com/Ermin Gutenberger, p. 61; © Alex Wong/Getty Images, p. 69; © Tony Barson/WireImage/Getty Images, p. 70 (top); AP Photo/Chad Harder, p. 70 (center); AP Photo/David Zalubowski, p. 71 (top); Photo Courtesy of U.S. Army, p. 71 (bottom); © Todd Strand/Independent Picture Service, pp. 72–73.

Front Cover: © offiwent.com/Alamy (left), © Sue Bennett/Alamy (top right), © LWA/Larry Williams/Blend Images/Getty Images (bottom right).

ABOUT THE AUTHOR

A graduate of Swarthmore College, Liz Sonneborn has written more than seventy books for children and adults, including *The American West, A to Z of American Indian Women, Wilma Mankiller, New York Public Library's Amazing Native American History,* and *Chronology of American Indian History*. In addition, she authored several titles for Lerner's Native American Histories series.